VANGUARD SERIES
EDITOR: MARTIN WINDROW

US LIGHT TANKS 1944-84

M24 CHAFFEE, M41 WALKER BULLDOG AND M551 SHERIDAN

Text by STEVEN J. ZALOGA

Colour plates by TERRY HADLER

OSPREY PUBLISHING LONDON

Published in 1984 by
Osprey Publishing Ltd
Member company of the George Philip Group
12–14 Long Acre, London WC2E 9LP
© Copyright 1984 Osprey Publishing Ltd

This book is copyrighted under the Berne Convention. All rights reserved. Apart from any fair dealing for the purpose of private study, research, criticism or review, as permitted under the Copyright Act, 1956, no part of this publication may be reproduced, stored in a retrieval system, or transmitted in any form or by any means, electronic, electrical, chemical, mechanical, optical, photocopying, recording or otherwise, without the prior permission of the copyright owner. Enquiries should be addressed to the Publishers.

British Library Cataloguing in Publication Data

Zaloga, Steven J.
　US light tanks 1944–84.
　1. Tanks (Military science)—United States—History
　I. Title
　623.74′752′0973　UG446.5

　ISBN 0 85045 541 3

Filmset in Great Britain
Printed in Hong Kong

Author's Note
The author would like to express his gratitude to Lt. Col. James Loop (USA Retd), Pierre Touzin, George Balin and Simon Dunstan for their generous help in collecting photographs and illustrative material used in the preparation of this book.

The M24 saw extensive combat in the final months of the Second World War. Here, infantry ride a Chaffee of the 20th Armd. Div. into Salzburg, Austria, on 4 May 1945, past the burning hulks of two German Bergepanthers. (US Army)

Wartime Roots

During the Second World War the principal light tanks of the US Army were the M3A1 and M5A1, popularly called the Stuarts. Initially, American tank battalions were configured either as light or medium tank battalions, equipped entirely with Stuart light tanks or M3 or M4 medium tanks. However, battlefield experience in North Africa made it quite clear that the light tank battalions were a liability. Their 37mm gun was inadequate against German tanks of the period, and really not very useful against unarmoured targets like entrenched troops. Their armour could be penetrated by nearly every available enemy anti-tank weapon, and offered little more than protection from small arms. Only their exceptional mobility was prized.

Many tank officers who had served in light tank battalions urged that the M3A1 and M5 be withdrawn from service in favour of uniform use of the M4 Sherman in tank battalions. This viewpoint became more and more diluted as it worked its way up the chain of command. In contrast to the company and battalion commanders whose opinions were formed primarily by disastrous battlefield experiences in North Africa, the generals serving with the Headquarters Armored Force and Headquarters Army Ground Forces were constantly badgered by industry and government officials who were opposed to terminating M5 production. These officials were concerned that such termination would jeopardise efforts to reach very high production goals for US tanks, since the factories producing the small and simple M5 light tank could not readily be converted to Sherman production. The high production goals had been set because the US tank industry was producing armoured vehicles not only for the US armed forces (which absorbed only about half of production), but also for the Allies under the Lend-Lease programme. The staff officers tried to accommodate these contradictory attitudes by re-organising US tank battalions in 1943 into a single type: each had only a single light company, and three companies of M4 mediums. Production plans for the M5 were trimmed back accordingly.

A replacement for the M5, the M7 light tank, was

3

Compared to the M5A1 Stuart, its predecessor in the light tank role, the M24 was spacious. This is the loader's station in a Chaffee turret, to the right of the 75mm M6 gun; the gunner's sight can be seen on the far side of the breech. (Zaloga)

ready for production in 1943. However, complaints about the M5's lack of armour and firepower had led to constant uparmouring and other improvements on the M7, which resulted in a vehicle nearly as heavy and costly as the M4 medium, but without its combat utility. As a result, the M5A1 light tank remained in production, much to the chagrin of the troops who were obliged to use it. Work shifted to a new light tank design, based on the fleet and highly successful M18 Hellcat tank destroyer. This resulted in 1944 in the M24 Chaffee light tank, named after the founder of the US Armored Force, Gen. Adna Chaffee.

The tactical employment of US light tanks was summarised in one of the armoured division training circulars: 'the light tank company provides a fast, mobile element that may be used to exploit the success of the medium tank (companies), to execute battle reconnaissance, or to act as a covering force for the (tank) battalion.' This doctrine stands in contrast to German or British practice, where armoured cars were the primary means of tactical reconnaissance. The US Army, like the Soviet Army, preferred tracked armoured vehicles due to their better battlefield mobility in poor terrain and seasonal conditions. While all parties agreed on high mobility as a prime requirement for light tanks, the US Army tactical doctrine raised serious problems for US tank designers.

On the one hand, the reconnaissance role did not demand a major calibre gun, since it was not the intention of recon units to fight their way through enemy lines for information, but to obtain it by speed and stealth. Nevertheless, the fact that a quarter of a tank battalion's armoured strength was made up of light tanks meant that the tactical doctrine also stressed the applicability of the light tank to flank security and exploitation, two roles where firepower was required. The M5's 37mm gun clearly did not satisfy these requirements, nor did the 57mm gun on the M7. As a result, the M6 75mm gun—a lightweight gun developed originally for B-25 Mitchell gunship bombers—was chosen for the new M24 light tank.

Curiously enough, the Soviets reached a similar conclusion in the design of their K-90 light tank in 1944–45, which was armed with a 76mm gun. This later resulted in the PT-76 amphibious light tank. Meanwhile the Germans, who did not saddle their light scout tanks with subsidiary roles like the US or Soviet armies, adopted in 1944 the Lynx scout tank, armed only with a 20mm gun. A specialised scout tank like the Lynx was an extravagance the Germans could ill afford in 1944, and few were built. In contrast, the general purpose light tanks like the American M24 and Soviet PT-76, while

After the war the M24s remained on duty in Germany with the Constabulary—each regiment had one troop of Chaffees. The Constabulary marking was a white disc with a blue inner ring and a blue central 'C' crossed by a lightning-bolt in red—see the bow of this tank. (National Archives)

The first US tank in action in Korea in 1950 was REBEL'S ROOST, a Chaffee of the Reconnaissance Company of the 24th Infantry Division; the engagement, against T-34/85s of the North Korean 105th Armd. Bde., took place at Chonui on 10 July. The front fenders of this tank bore the white codes '24X', '24-R21'; white national stars on the turret side and glacis were obscured with mud. See also Vanguard 27, *Armour of the Korean War.* **(US Army)**

perhaps not entirely satisfactory in any one of their several roles, still had a greater utility overall, and were built in correspondingly large numbers.

Because of the delay brought about by the failure of the M7 project, an M5A1 replacement was not available until late in 1944, and the M5A1 remained the most numerous US light tank in the tank battalions at the end of the Second World War. The first M24 was produced in April 1944, and the first batch of M24s began to be issued to troops in the ETO in December 1944 during the fighting in the Ardennes. The M24 saw no fighting in the Pacific theatre.

The M24 was very favourably received by the tankers of the armoured divisions, independent tank battalions, and cavalry recon squadrons lucky enough to be allotted them in place of the M5A1. The Chaffee was roomier, and had distinctly better firepower. It was still too thinly armoured to withstand tank gun or anti-tank fire; but by the end of 1944 most tank battalions had learned to use their older M5A1s circumspectly to minimise the danger presented by their thin armour, and the M24 would be used in a similar fashion. In the armoured divisions, a very popular role for the light tanks was their use in support of the half-tracks of the mechanised infantry. Since the half-tracks were also thinly armoured, it was easier to employ these vehicles in a harmonious fashion with the light tanks. Nevertheless, it would probably be accurate to say that most tankers would have preferred four companies of M4 mediums rather than three of mediums and one of light tanks, even the improved M24 light tank. By 1944–45 heavy calibre anti-tank guns, Panzerfausts, and other weapons were available in such numbers to the German Army (as compared to their relative shortage in 1940–41, when light tank doctrine was first espoused) that one must question the utility of light tanks for any role other than scouting. Nevertheless, the M24 remained in production, and up to June 1945, 4,415 were built.

An M24 and an M46 medium tank of the 64th Medium Tank Battalion support 3rd Inf. Div. troops during fighting in Korea, 18 February 1952. By this stage of the war the M46 and M4 had taken over the bulk of the armoured task because of the inadequacies of the M24 in a role for which it was never designed. (US Army)

The low-velocity M6 gun of the M24 gave it very little anti-tank value against contemporary German tanks. It could not penetrate any of the major types frontally, and was successful only in certain side or rear shots at close range. The gun was really intended to deal with unarmoured targets like trucks, buildings, and entrenched troops. It used the same ammunition as the 75mm gun in the M4 Sherman, and therefore had a useful HE round. There were occasional fluke successes against Panzers, however. For example, in early March of 1945, some M24s of Troop F, 4th Cavalry Recon Squadron blundered into a pair of Tigers outside Domagen, Germany. Both sides were equally surprised at the encounter; but the M24s had the advantage of faster turret traverse, and before the Germans could swing their large, clumsy turrets at their bantamweight foes, the M24s slammed several HE rounds against the side and rear turret armour of the Tigers. The rounds did not penetrate, but detonated internal ammunition and stores which burned both tanks out. This incident hardly inspired other M24 crews to go Tiger-hunting; but it did accent the fact that paper calculations cannot absolutely predict the outcome of tank battles, due to the vagaries of circumstance, luck, and crew performance.

During the war a small quantity of M24s were provided to Britain and the Soviet Union. After the war a very large percentage of M24s were turned over to many foreign armies, where they formed the kernel of new armoured units. In the US Army the most active use of the M24 was in the ten light tank troops attached to the US Constabulary Regiments which were used for policing duties in Germany.

The M24 in Korea

The hasty postwar demobilisation of the US Army left it ill-prepared to cope with the crisis brought about by the invasion of South Korea in the summer of 1950. Although there were four tank battalions assigned to the four infantry divisions on occupation duty in Japan, these battalions in fact had only a single 'A' Company each, with about 17 M24 Chaffee light tanks. The battalions had not been given the heavier M4A3E8 Shermans due to fear that they would damage Japanese roads and light bridges. The infantry divisions also had an organic reconnaissance company each, with a further 17 Chaffees. These tanks were rushed to Korea and constituted almost the only US armour available until M4s and M26s began to arrive in August.

The M24 was never designed to engage enemy medium tanks, and was no match for the dreaded T-34/85. On 10 July 1950 the first armour engagement of the war was fought between several M24s of the 24th Recon Company and some T-34/85s of the 105th North Korean Armoured Brigade. Two M24s were lost, but, much to the Chaffee crews' credit, a single T-34/85 was destroyed. Nevertheless, it was only the arrival of heavier US tanks that stemmed the tide of North Korean armour. The M24 continued to serve in light tank companies of the tank battalions in Korea, and also with divisional reconnaissance companies up to 1953. (See also Vanguard 27, *Armour of the Korean War*.)

A Chaffee named EAGLE CLAW routs out snipers: Korea, 20 May 1951. Although useless against the Communist T-34/85s, the M24 was still effective in support of infantry against enemy troops lacking anti-tank weapons. (US Army)

Another Replacement

The rising temperature of the Cold War after 1947 led the US Army to re-evaluate its plans for armoured units. After the painfully obvious lessons of 1942–45, the Army finally decided to remove light tank companies from the tank battalions, which would now be composed entirely of medium tanks. Instead, each armoured division would have a reconnaissance battalion with 30 light tanks; and a further 28 dispersed among divisional units, three to each combat command for scouting, and two to each tank battalion and armoured infantry battalion. These plans did not come about until 1952, and were not universal in the battalions fighting in Korea.

Besides their use in light tank companies, the light tanks of the Second World War had been used in mechanised cavalry units. Although ostensibly designed for scouting, postwar studies found that in 1942–45 such units were used in defensive combat

An M24 of the 79th Tank Bn. patrols the perimeter of Kimpo Airbase in February 1951. Note fluorescent orange air identification panel stretched over the turret roof. (US Army)

33 per cent of the time; on special operations (such as mobile reserve or rear area clean-up) 29 per cent of the time; on security duty (such as flank protection of other units) 25 per cent of the time; on offensive operations 10 per cent of the time; and on scouting (their main tactical role), only 3 per cent of the time. This had serious implications for light tank design. While Army tacticians had been willing to retain light tanks if used primarily for scouting, it was evident from the study that they were in fact used mainly in other roles for which they were not entirely suited. There remained a consensus that a light, mobile scouting tank was needed to equip the new reconnaissance battalions; but the Army had finally come around to the conclusion that the scout tank should be armed with a gun sufficient to defeat the enemy armour that was likely to be encountered when the light tank was used in its other, non-scouting roles. The M24 was not capable of mounting a much heavier weapon, so a complete redesign was required. Although the new tank was not to be significantly different from the M24 in armour or mobility, it would have enhanced firepower.

The project was initiated in July 1946 and the vehicle was designated the T37. A secondary consideration in the programme was the develop-

The ROK Army began to receive M24s in 1953: this tank served with the South Korean Tank Training Center at Kwang-ju—see Plate B2. (US Army)

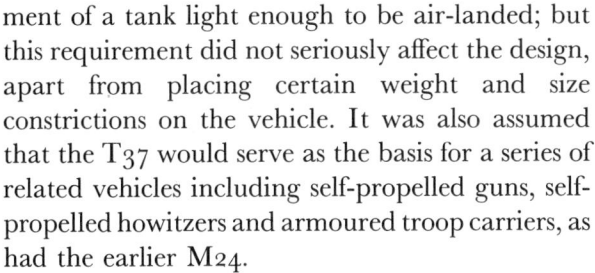

ment of a tank light enough to be air-landed; but this requirement did not seriously affect the design, apart from placing certain weight and size constrictions on the vehicle. It was also assumed that the T37 would serve as the basis for a series of related vehicles including self-propelled guns, self-propelled howitzers and armoured troop carriers, as had the earlier M24.

The T37 incorporated electric turret traverse, an optical rangefinder, and power elevation for the gun. The development programme envisioned design of three turrets, each with increasing levels of sophistication. The Phase 2 turret added the improved T91 76mm gun, and a gun stabilisation system developed by Vickers; and the Phase 3 turret was to feature automatic loading. Due to the differences between the Phase 1 and Phase 2 turrets, it was decided to change the designation of the tank with the Phase 2 turret to T41. The 76mm gun was designed to be capable of defeating the Soviet T-34/85, by then the standard tank in the Soviet arsenal.

Prototypes of the T41 were completed in 1949, and the tank entered trials. Some concern was voiced over the very high cost of the tank, due to its expensive optical rangefinder and other advanced features. This led to the development of a lower-cost turret, which was fitted to the T41E1 prototype. Further work led to the addition of a new hydraulic turret traverse system to replace the electric traverse on the T41E1, resulting in the T41E2. Trials of both vehicles proved successful. Due to post-war scrapping of much equipment the US Army was desperate for new tanks, and authorised Cadillac to begin building the T41E1 even before it was type classified. The first T41E1s were produced in mid-1951 and were issued to the troops later in the year. A total of 1,802 T41E1s were completed before production shifted to the improved T41E2. Finally, in May 1953, the two versions were type classified as M41 and M41A1. In a complete change from earlier practices, the new tank was nicknamed 'Little Bulldog', instead of after a famous US general. However, it was decided in 1951 to name the tank after Gen. W. W. Walker, after his fatal jeep accident in Korea. This resulted in the unusual name of the Walker Bulldog tank. It is interesting to note that in November 1950 the Army officially changed the designation of the T41 from 'light tank' to '76mm gun combat tank'. This made the M24 the last tank officially designated a light tank in the US Army—though the term 'light tank' is still used here as a useful method to distinguish between main battle tanks and their smaller brethren.

The M41 proved very popular in service with US armoured and armoured cavalry units. It was fast, nimble and responsive: three characteristics much cherished in a scout tank. The gun was adequate to deal with the T-34/85; but by the time the M41 finally arrived on the scene, the T-54 had appeared, which greatly reduced the utility of the M41 in tank combat. Some former M41 crewmen complained that the turret was rather cramped due to all the equipment associated with the turret traverse, stabilisation and gun. A more worrying feature was the risk posed to the driver when riding with his head out of the hatch: should the gun traverse leftwards without the driver being warned, serious head injuries could occur. The M41 was also a very noisy tank, having a very loud, whining engine. This was not greatly appreciated by reconnaissance crews; but the peppy performance of the engine certainly was! Like many US tanks of the period, the M41 and M41A1 had miserable gas mileage, but this was finally rectified in September 1956 with the development of a modified engine with fuel injection. New production tanks with the AOSI-895-5 engine were classified as M41A2, and older tanks with fuel injection kits added were classified as M41A3. Production of the M41 and its subvariants totalled about 5,500 tanks before production ceased in the late 1950s.

Chaffee of 81st Recon, 1st Armd. Div. in New Mexico in 1952; these tanks began to be replaced by the new M41 the following year. The turret marking, in yellow, identifies 'A' Co. in the British manner; below it is the name ANADARKO. (US Army)

As mentioned above, the 1952 re-organisation of the US armoured divisions placed the bulk of the division's M41s in the divisional reconnaissance battalion, with 30 tanks. The remaining 28 tanks were scattered as scout tanks among the division's other battalions. The shift to the 'pentatonic' organisation in 1957–59 dropped the total number of M41s in an armoured division to 54 tanks. The ROAD re-organisation of 1962–64 had more substantial impact. The total number of M41s was reduced to 40: 18 in a divisional armoured cavalry squadron, and two in each of the tank and mechanised infantry battalions. There were also substantial modifications within the armoured cavalry units.

Shortly before M41 production ceased, the engineer teams at the Detroit Arsenal began development of a 90mm smooth-bore gun version of the M41, called the T49. Although two prototypes were completed, no actual production took place.

Nor was the further development of the M41 the only route pursued. In February 1953 plans began for development of a new light tank, much smaller and less expensive than the M41, designated the T71. This was armed with the same gun as the M41. No production of this type ensued, because in 1954 the Army gave AAI Inc. permission to go ahead with their own conception of a new light tank of a radically novel design, which was built in prototype form as the T92. The main attraction of the T92 was that it was lighter and smaller than the M41. Although the M41 was air-transportable, it was not suited for paradropping. With interest growing during the mid-1950s in rapid deployment of US divisions to crisis areas, a configuration such as the

Although the M41 quickly replaced the M24 in armoured units, the Chaffee soldiered on in other organisations. This one served with the 196th Regimental Combat Team at Ft. Richardson, Alaska, in June 1954. Beneath the name CLEO is the yellow/blue/red Armor triangle insignia. (US Army)

T92 was much discussed. The main drawback was the growing realisation that the 76mm gun on the T92 was not really adequate to handle standard Soviet tanks like the T-54, and that a 90mm gun was too heavy for the chassis. Series production of the T92 was not authorised.

The M551 Sheridan

By the late 1950s, Army planners had come to realise that the M41 was suffering from the traditional light tank problem: inadequate firepower against contemporary main battle tanks.

An M24 'Bison' of the French 1er Régiment de Chasseurs à Cheval on patrol in Indo-China during 1953: compare with Plate A2. The turret side sports the beautiful full-colour regimental badge; the name OUDENARDE and number 'IC-93015' are painted in white on black strips on the glacis plate. Note that by this date most French units had a proportion of locally recruited personnel. The M24's low ground pressure made it manoeuvrable even in the marshly terrain of Tonkin. (ECPA)

Unfortunately, the obvious solution of using a larger calibre gun had many drawbacks. Most importantly, the larger the gun, the heavier the basic chassis required. The inevitable weight connected with the heavier gun would also doom Army hopes to employ such a vehicle in an airborne role using parachutes. These two seemingly incompatible requirements—light weight to allow the use of a new light tank in airborne divisions, and a larger gun for more adequate anti-tank performance—nearly put an end to any hope for a future light tank. However, in January 1959, concept studies began of a revolutionary new system which seemed to outflank these traditional light tank problems.

Instead of using a conventional rifled gun, with its resultant heavy recoil forces, a novel gun/missile launcher was suggested. The main anti-tank round would be a small guided missile, which would impart only modest recoil forces against the chassis, and consequently would not demand the use of a particularly large or heavy tank. This guided round would give the light tank superior anti-tank performance to most contemporary large-calibre guns, in terms of both penetration and long-range accuracy, albeit at a high cost per round. To keep costs down, the high explosive round would be a conventional gun-fired projectile. The system was codenamed Shillelagh, and it was planned to incorporate it on the new light tank; on a new version of the M60 tank; and on the new main battle tank, the MBT-70.

The new light tank was given the forbidding acronym AR/AAV, or Armored Reconnaissance/Airborne Assault Vehicle, XM551. In 1960 General Motors was selected to develop the tank itself; and in 1961 the first test firings of the Shillelagh took place, using an XM551 testbed turret on an M41 hull. The Shillelagh development programme would turn out to be one of the most complicated and controversial tank development efforts of the 1960s, contributing to the demise of the MBT-70 programme, and having serious repercussions on the deployment of the M551 tank.

The problems stemmed from the over-ambitious nature of certain aspects of the programme. Not only was the US Army planning on developing a radically new type of gun/missile launcher; it was also intending to field for the first time a fully 'self-consuming' projectile casing. The requirement for this feature stemmed from the fact that the Shillelagh was to be employed on the MBT-70. The MBT-70 was designed to permit its employment in a chemically contaminated environment, and the need to dispose of bulky spent brass projectile casings inside a cramped tank presented serious problems. Consumable casings, made of materials that would vaporise (except for a small brass end casing) when the gun was fired, offered the solution to this problem. Or so it was hoped. . .

In fact, the caseless ammunition was a source of constant problems. Tests of the conventional HE round showed that the cartridge was susceptible to

The Austrian Army used M24s alongside their Soviet-supplied T-34/85s into the 1960s. (Ostreich Heeresbild)

The combination of a Belgian M24, British-outfitted infantry, and a roadsign still bullet-holed from the 1944–45 fighting gives a weird time-warp quality to this shot of joint Belgian-Dutch training exercises in August 1951. (US Army)

humidity, which distorted the casing shape and made it impossible to chamber properly. Some rounds that *were* chambered had absorbed so much moisture that the casing did not completely burn away. As a result, when the next round was chambered, it would occasionally spontaneously detonate on contact with burning remnants of the previous casing still in the gun barrel—with results which may be imagined. Ironically, the design of the sophisticated anti-tank missile round, the MGM-51A, went more smoothly, although its reliability remained low. The design of the tank itself also went relatively smoothly; and in April 1965 the first contract was issued for initial limited production of the XM551 Sheridan, even though the ammunition problems had not been completely solved.

The haste with which the Sheridan was put into production further complicated the ammunition problems by placing even greater pressure on the design teams to rectify this nearly intractable problem. Tanks were completed but could not be deployed, due both to the lack of the new ammunition and to modifications which were shown to be needed by further field testing of the gun system. The Sheridan controversy became a

Army decided instead to add an open-breech scavenger system to the gun after several hundred M551s had been completed. This system blew air into the gun tube, in the hope of clearing it of any burning residue.

In February 1967 the system was added to new production Sheridans even before it had been fully tested. The first tests took place at the Panama Tropic Test Center in the spring of 1967—and proved disastrous. The new open-bore system blew flaming debris back into the turret, threatening to detonate stored ammunition rounds. The smoke and fumes were severe enough to prevent the gunner from sighting through the fire control devices. So much carbon monoxide was created, and not expelled by the firing, that it was noted that even the driver became glassy-eyed and slurred in his speech—classic symptoms of carbon monoxide poisoning. Of the Panama firings, 39 per cent left flaming or smouldering debris in the breech and gun tube. In April 1967 orders were rushed out forbidding units to store more than a single round of caseless ammunition in tanks for fear of internal brew-ups. Nevertheless, the Sheridan remained in production with this same unsatisfactory open breech scavenger system! It was not until October 1967 that production of the Sheridans with open-breech scavengers was terminated. Sheridans continued to roll off the assembly line incomplete until January 1968, when a closed-breech scavenger system was adopted. The new system blew compressed air down the tube with a closed breech, preventing the entrance of smouldering debris and gasses into the fighting compartment.

From March to June a production Sheridan was tested in Panama to determine whether the vehicle was suitable even ignoring the gun problems. The tests revealed excessive engine overheating, extreme engine noise, firing circuit problems, leaking recoil systems and an unreliable gun. During trials of the missile rounds, only two out of 13 were considered hits. This led the Test and Evaluation Command to consider developing a metallic case for the round, or even dropping the troublesome 152mm gun/missile system in favour of a low-recoil 105mm howitzer. However, in October 1968 the metallic case option was cancelled due to incompatibility with the MBT-70 tank, and efforts were directed at a second-generation combustible case.

major source of bickering within the Army between the developing agencies, which continued to back the programme and to promise quick rectification of the problems, and the agencies representing the units in the field, which were reluctant to see any further production until a satisfactory conventional round was developed.

The development agencies won out, and type classification of the Sheridan as the M551 was approved in May 1966. Several new types of coatings were tested on the ammunition in an effort to rectify the moisture problems, but none were satisfactory. Finally, a plastic cover bag was developed to seal the round until it was ready to be fired. Even this was not entirely satisfactory, and the

While these tests were going on, a parallel series of trials were conducted by the Australian Army, which was considering the Sheridan for its own use. The Australians found many of the same problems as those highlighted by the US tests, particularly stressing the lack of range of the conventional round, the poor engine cooling system and deficiencies in the gunner's sight. The Australian Minister for the Army rejected the Sheridan on the grounds that it was 'unsuitable for Vietnam-type conflicts—the only kind of war in which Australia is likely to be involved in the foreseeable future'—a prescient comment, indeed. Nor did the Sheridan perform much better in the other extreme. Arctic tests in Alaska in May 1968 led the Test Center to recommend that the Sheridan not be used in arctic winter conditions.

Tests on the new closed-breech scavenging system (CBSS) and a new neoprene bag for the ammunition showed that both techniques substantially reduced the residue problems, but that the CBSS suffered from operational unreliability. Small numbers of Sheridans finally made their way into the hands of troops in 1968, mainly for trials purposes. A large proportion were inoperable on any given day, due to severe maintenance and reliability problems and the lack of personnel with maintenance training for the complex turret systems. The two worst problems were the firing circuit and the recoil system. The recoil system had a propensity to leak due to the enormous forces built up on it when firing the conventional HE round. The recoil from the conventional round was enough to lift the front of the tank a foot-and-a-half off the ground and smash the entire vehicle a few feet rearward. The crews had to be specifically warned to brace themselves before a round was fired to prevent serious injury.

A Chaffee of the Norwegian Panserkolen on exercise in the 1950s. These tanks were rebuilt in the 1970s, and are still in service! (National Archives)

An M24 of the Pakistani 29th Cavalry is inspected by Indian soldiers after the 1971 war. The Chaffee was hopelessly obsolete by the time it faced India's modern Soviet tanks. White turret bands were used by Pakistan as a quick identification—they had tank types in common with their enemy. This M24 is camouflaged with swathes of grey over an olive drab base coat.

The Sheridan in Vietnam

As the Australian Army had noted, the Sheridan was unsuitable for Vietnam-type conditions. US field commanders in Vietnam agreed, noting that the continued reliability problems of the various systems made them very reluctant to accept any Sheridans except on a test basis. Moreover, since the Sheridan had been designed mainly for Europe, with a strong emphasis on anti-tank performance, no anti-personnel round had been developed for the main gun. An anti-tank round was useless in Vietnam, while the available HE round for the Sheridan had no particular advantages over the 90mm HE round used by M48A3 Pattons. Nevertheless, the development agencies in the US were anxious to deploy the Sheridan to Vietnam, in hopes that a display of its virtues would mollify the growing number of critics in the US Congress (and within the Army itself). The new XM625 'Beehive' round was developed specifically for Vietnam. It contained 9,900 tiny flechettes, and was gruesomely effective against unprotected troops.

The development agencies again had their way; and in January 1969, 64 Sheridans were shipped to Vietnam for the 1st Squadron, 11th Armored Cavalry and the 3rd Squadron, 4th Armored Cavalry. In February the first M551 was lost to a mine which caused the caseless ammunition to explode, killing the driver. Such a mine would only have blown a wheel off an M48A3 Patton without penetrating the hull; and while it would have caused comparable structural damage to an M113, there would not have been the problem of stored ammunition 'cooking off'. The report on the incident was extremely critical of the fact that side appliqué had already been developed which might have prevented the caseless ammunition rupture

17

France was the biggest user of the M24 after the US Army itself. These tanks, marked with the names of provinces, cities and battles in the usual French manner, are parading in February 1955 to commemorate the tenth anniversary of the battle of Colmar. (US Army)

which led to the internal fires which destroyed the tank.

The ammunition proved very fragile in the humid conditions of Vietnam, as the field commanders had feared. During the first three months of use, 140 rounds were found to be damaged, mainly by mine shock (from anti-personnel mines!) and even from cross-country travel. Another 41 rounds misfired due to casing distortion, amounting to about one round in every 50 fired. This was extremely aggravating to the crews' as these misfires almost invariably occurred in the heat of combat, and the rounds were extremely difficult to extract from the gun tube. The Sheridans' engines failed repeatedly due to clogging of radiators and air filters in dusty and jungle conditions. As the Australians had noted a year before, the fan pulley was shoddy and caused

When replaced in South Vietnamese armoured units by M41s, many M24s had their engines removed and were turned into static pillboxes. Some were retained by the South Vietnamese Air Force as anti-coup security for Premier Ky, and were used to patrol the perimeter of Tan Son Nhut Airbase. See Plate C1. (US Army)

air cooling failures. The solution developed by the Australians—substitution of a sturdier steel pulley—was instituted only after repeated complaints by the US crews.

The most common failure in the Sheridan was turret electrical power failures, and the recoil troubles noted in Stateside tests again occurred with alarming frequency in Vietnam. As if these vices were not enough, the turret in the Sheridan was very cramped and prone to overheating, which was a serious difficulty in Vietnam's tropical climate.

Aside from crew dissatisfaction with the vehicle's durability, the results of the initial deployment were contradictory. The 3/4th Cavalry, which had switched from the sturdy M48A3 to the flimsy M551, particularly disliked the Sheridan after the February mine incident. In contrast, the 1/11th Armored Cavalry, which had switched from M113 ACAVs to the Sheridan, liked the M551 for its considerable increase in firepower. On the basis of the 11ACR recommendation more M551s were shipped to Vietnam, totalling about 200 by the end of the year. Eventually, most of the US armoured cavalry units in Vietnam were equipped with the Sheridan.

The M551 never earned the full trust of its crews in Vietnam. It did not have the jungle-crunching ability of the M48A3 when in dense vegetation; and though it was comparable in mobility to the M113, it had neither its durability nor reliability. Its main advantage over the M113 was its firepower. But even this advantage was degraded, as some crews grew fearful of the mine risk posed by the caseless ammunition and carried very few rounds, preferring turret-mounted machine guns. It should be recorded that other crews used the vehicle very successfully, appreciating both its advantages and its drawbacks.

To help solve the mine problem, titanium armour panels were attached under the bow of the M551, with partial success. Sheridan crews quickly learned that an RPG-7 impact could lead to secondary internal explosions of ruptured ammunition, and therefore abandoned tanks quickly when hit. In contrast, M48 tank crews frequently remained in their tanks due to the relatively low risk

The NM-116, the Norwegian Army's extensively rebuilt M24 derivative; it has a new engine, a new 90mm gun, a laser rangefinder and other fire control improvements. (Norwegian Army)

of secondary internal detonations. One of the worst features of the Sheridan was its electrical system, which often malfunctioned during Vietnam's rainy seasons, sometimes with tragic results. One M551 troop escorting an M113 unit along a road was the victim of such an occurrence. Many Sheridan crews so feared the likelihood of a catastrophic explosion from mines or RPG-7s that they rode on the outside of the vehicle. Some of the crews then rigged external controls so that the main gun could be fired from outside the vehicle. In this particular case, the M551 had a flechette round chambered and ready to fire in case the convoy was ambushed. The crew had the turret pointed forward when an electrical malfunction accidentally triggered the gun, spraying the exposed troops riding on the top of an M113 in front of it with a lethal hailstorm.

The M551 was not only unpopular; it was also a terribly costly vehicle for use in Vietnam. The everpresent enemy mines had a particularly unfortunate result if large enough to rip open the hull. But even small anti-personnel mines that were too small to cause terminal damage often tore up the aluminium armour of the vehicle so badly that it was essentially unrepairable. Many M551s were simply blown up in place rather than waste time

In the 1950s light tanks were finally removed from US tank battalions and concentrated in reconnaissance companies. This M41 of the 7th Recon Co., 7th Inf. Div. was photographed in May 1955 during exercises in Korea. (US Army)

An M41 Walker Bulldog of the 2nd Armored Cavalry Regiment exercises at Ft. Meade, Maryland, with an M48 Patton: April 1957. (US Army)

trying to repair them. At the time an M551 cost about $300,000, as compared to about $15,000 for an M113 ACAV.

The development of the M551 was a horrible example of mismanagement and bureaucratic bungling. While it should have been expected that so radically novel a design would be very time-consuming to develop and field, the tank was put into production prematurely before essential problems had been solved. Moreover, rather than slowing or temporarily halting production once serious shortcomings were discovered, production continued, requiring later and costly retrofit programmes. More disturbing was the careless and unnecessary deployment of the Sheridan to Vietnam, where its main advantage—its tremendous anti-tank firepower—was largely irrelevant, but where the climate ensured that all of its technical shortcomings would become most manifest.

The M551 débâcle had long-term consequences as well. The Sheridan fiasco, and the related horror stories about the M60A2 and MBT-70, soured Congress on the subject of future Army armoured vehicle programmes. Even though the Army substantially altered its testing and verification policies after the Sheridan programme, Congress remained very cynical of any Army statements regarding the outcome of its vehicle testing programmes. As a result of this understandable reaction, in the late 1970s Congress came near to killing the much-needed M1 Abrams main battle tank. Although the M1 had been tested more thoroughly than any tank in history and had not suffered any particularly serious development problems, the US Congress was so sceptical of Army honesty over the test results that it came very near to not providing funding for the procurement of the new tank. The mismanagement of the M551 programme created an attitude in Congress which seriously jeopardised programmes which followed, and this attitude has still not entirely dissipated to this day.

When the Sheridan was finally issued to cavalry units in Germany and the United States in the early 1970s, many of its problems had been resolved. The vehicle was popular with the cavalry troops for its firepower and for its peppy performance. In a European climate the ammunition problems were nowhere near as severe as in Vietnam, and nor were the electrical system problems. The main drawback remained the severe recoil when firing the 152mm

'Light' tank or not, it is not smart for an automobile to mess with an M41—as this hapless vehicle discovered in Saigon during the 1968 Tet fighting. The M41A3 was the standard tank of the ARVN until the early 1970s, when the US supplied some M48A3 Pattons.

main gun with caseless ammunition rounds such as the XM409E5 HEAT, XM657E2 HE, XM625 canister or XM411E3 training round. These rounds hurled the tank about, loosened components, injured crews and caused misalignment of the fire control system. This led to its occasional nickname—'The Plastic Tank'.

A total of 1,700 M551s were completed between 1966 and 1970, and over 100 were lost in Vietnam. In 1971 an AN/VVG-1 laser rangefinder and other improvements were added to the M551, resulting in the M551A1. Initially the Army planned to use the M551 chassis as the basis for a whole series of new self-propelled guns, air defence vehicles and other armoured support vehicles, but the problems with the chassis led to cancellation of these schemes.

The M551 was issued to armoured cavalry squadrons, armour battalions attached to airborne units, and armoured cavalry regiments. The ACR had 84 Sheridans—three at regimental HQ and 27 in each of the three cavalry squadrons. The cavalry squadrons had three troops, each with nine M551s. The 4/64th Armor, attached to the 82nd Airborne Division, had 54 M551s, three at battalion HQ and three companies each with 17 Sheridans. In addition to these units built around the Sheridan, armoured brigades had nine for reconnaissance duties.

Although designed for use both as an airborne tank and as a cavalry scout tank, the M551 was seldom used in its airborne role except by 4/64th Armor. The Sheridan is not actually parachuted, but rather is 'LAPESed' (low altitude parachute extraction system). The tank is carried in a transport aircraft (usually the C-130 Hercules) lashed to a fibreboard pallet. The transport makes a low, slow pass over the landing zone, and a drogue chute is released which drags the Sheridan out of the aircraft. The cardboard pallet absorbs much of the impact. The crew is parachuted separately from the tank, and, after removing the attachment straps, can drive the tank away.

After hardly a decade of service, the US Army decided in 1978 to retire most of the M551 Sheridans from the armoured cavalry. The continuing problems with the recoil system and ammunition had caused intractable maintenance difficulties. In armoured cavalry regiments the M551 was initially replaced by the M60, and in some other cavalry units by the M113. The only units to retain the M551 are the 4/46th Armor, attached to the 82nd Airborne Division, and a troop of 12 M551s in the Tennessee National Guard. It was a sad demise for an ambitious and revolutionary tank design. No other light tank had been so formidably armed, and perhaps none ever will be again.

Taiwan was among the many nations to receive the M41 under the US Military Assistance Program in the 1950s; it replaced the earlier M5A1 in Nationalist Chinese service.

Another Cavalry Tank?

In 1971 the US Army initiated the ARSV (Armored Reconnaissance Scout Vehicle Program). The XM800 ARSV was intended mainly as a replacement for the M114, a shoddy little scout vehicle whose disreputable history has been forgotten if only because of the publicity attending the M551, M60A2 and MBT-70. Unlike the M551 Sheridan, the XM800 ARSV was intended as a pure scout vehicle with no real capability to serve in other roles where serious firepower would be needed. Two prototypes were built: a tracked light tank by FMC, and a wheeled armoured car derived from the Lockheed Twister programme. Both vehicles were small, fast and nimble, and armed only with a 20mm gun. In 1975 the ARSV programme was abandoned. Congress was in a very foul mood after the M551 programme, and was unenthusiastic when asked to fund yet another US Army armoured vehicle whose role was not clearly understood.

This forced the Armored Cavalry to begin thinking of other solutions to their vehicle predicament. The M551 was likely to be phased out due to its technical shortcomings, the M114 was already being phased out, and Congress seemed unlikely to permit development of a new vehicle. In 1977 Congress and the Department of Defense finally urged the Armored Cavalry to merge their requirements with the infantry, which was developing the new MICV infantry transporter. The result was the IFV/CFV (Infantry Fighting Vehicle/Cavalry Fighting Vehicle).

The MICV was to be armed only with a 25mm gun in a one-man turret. The cavalry insisted that a two-man turret be used to ensure better observation of the terrain, and that a TOW missile launcher be added. This peculiar hybrid gun/missile combination was first carried on the Soviet BMP in the early 1960s, and offered a different approach to the firepower dilemma that had haunted light tank designs like the M551. On the one hand, the TOW guided anti-tank missile could destroy any existing tank with great accuracy, and proved to be more reliable and effective than the Shillelagh missile

The Walker Bulldog replaced the Chaffee in Belgian service; this example bears the markings of the Belgian 1st Infantry Division. (Pierre Touzin)

system on the M551. On the other hand, the 25mm M242 Bushmaster autocannon could be used to attack 'soft' targets such as troops, trucks, buildings and lightly armoured vehicles, instead of the conventional high-explosive caseless rounds used on the M551. While not packing the explosive wallop of the Sheridan rounds, the rapid rate of fire makes the M242 a very lethal weapon against a wide range of targets (including attack helicopters), and has none of the debilitating recoil problems of the Sheridan gun/missile system. Development of the IFV/CFV was relatively untroubled, as the design is fairly conventional even if its tactical employment, especially in the infantry role, is quite revolutionary. (This issue will be examined in a forthcoming Vanguard.) The IFV/CFV was type classified as the M2 and M3, and production began in the early 1980s.

The M3 Cavalry Fighting Vehicle differs from its infantry counterpart mainly in the configuration of the internal stowage in the rear hull. Instead of carrying a squad of infantry, it carries two cavalry scouts and more ammunition. The M3 marks a fundamental shift away from light tanks, at least in name. The M3 is more clearly a derivation of infantry armoured transporter design than traditional light tank design, yet in a sense it represents an evolutionary convergence of the two concepts. On the one hand, armoured infantry transporters have become increasingly well armed, so that they do not require the services of a light tank to shepherd them to their objectives, as was the case in the Second World War. On the other hand, as these transporters have absorbed the role undertaken by the light tank companies of the old 1940s tank battalions, the resulting design has proved very adaptable to the requirements of a modern cavalry vehicle which stresses utility in a wide range of roles including scouting, flank security, patrol and defensive operations.

Light Tanks Forever?

Although the M3 CFV would seem to mark the end of the light tank in the US Army, this may not be the case. The Army had nearly 1,500 M551 Sheridans in mothballs in 1980. The basic automotive design is quite acceptable, even if the turret and gun system is suspect.

The first use to which these vehicles was put was that of training tank, or to use the official term, Opposing Force Vehicle, Full-Tracked, M551A2. The M551A2 designation applies to about 170 Sheridans which were converted to *ersatz* Soviet armoured vehicles in the early 1980s for use by the National Training Center in the deserts of southern California. The revival of the centre for live training of US ground forces stemmed from the outstanding results of training Air Force and Navy pilots in the 'Red Flag' exercises, where F-5 fighters were used to represent Soviet fighter units. The M551A2 units were configured as mock Soviet motor rifle regiments with a mixture of *ersatz* T-72s, BMPs and SO-152s, built on Sheridan chassis by means of sheet metal disguises. The vehicles were also fitted with a full range of laser training simulation devices from the MILES system. These consist of a laser 'gun' which can be fired at opposing tanks. Each of the tanks in the exercise is fitted with an array of laser detectors which can sense a 'hit' from the laser gun of another tank. This data is fed into a small micro-processor on the tank which evaluates whether the tank has been killed, near-missed or disabled. If killed, the system sets off a flashing 'bubble-gum' beacon and a smoke grenade, the tank's engine is automatically turned off and the laser gun rendered inoperative. This provides a remarkably realistic method of simulating combat, and is integrated with a similar system for small arms, anti-tank missiles and air defence weapons. The OPFOR's units at the NTC have developed a healthy reputation in the US Army as a crack outfit, and to date their M551A2 units have never lost a major engagement during the training manoeuvres.

The remaining M551s are likely to be utilised in a more bellicose fashion. Although the US Marines were reluctant to consider the M551s in a modified form for their Light Armored Vehicle requirement, some Army officers have been promoting the re-arming of the M551 as a light tank destroyer. The Army has a requirement for a Mobile Protected Gun (MPG) which is supposed to be satisfied in the short term by a derivative of the Marine LAV, the M1047—an eight-wheeled armoured car armed only with a 25mm gun. The vehicle is quite large and bulky since it was developed as a troop carrier. The main requirement for the vehicle is light weight to permit rapid deployment to crisis areas. Congress

1: M24, US 79th Tk. Bn.; Han River, Korea, 1950

2: M24, French 1er Régt. de Chasseurs à Cheval; Indo China, 1953

A

1: M24, 3rd Tk.Bn., Japanese GSDF, 1970

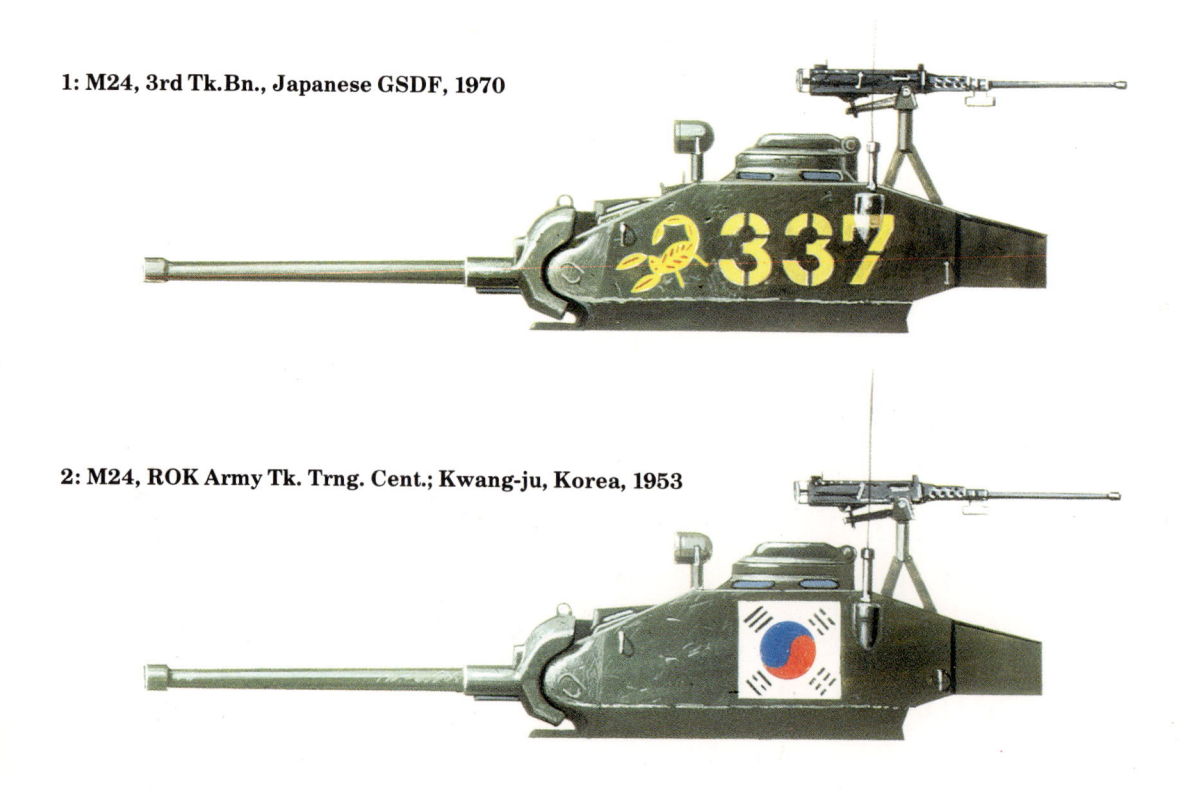

2: M24, ROK Army Tk. Trng. Cent.; Kwang-ju, Korea, 1953

3: M24, Esc. de M., 1er RCC; Dien Bien Phu, 1954

B

1: M24, RVNAF Security Flight; Tan Son Nhut, Vietnam, 1968

2: M24, Mecklenbourg Cavalry Regt.; Portugal, 1978

C

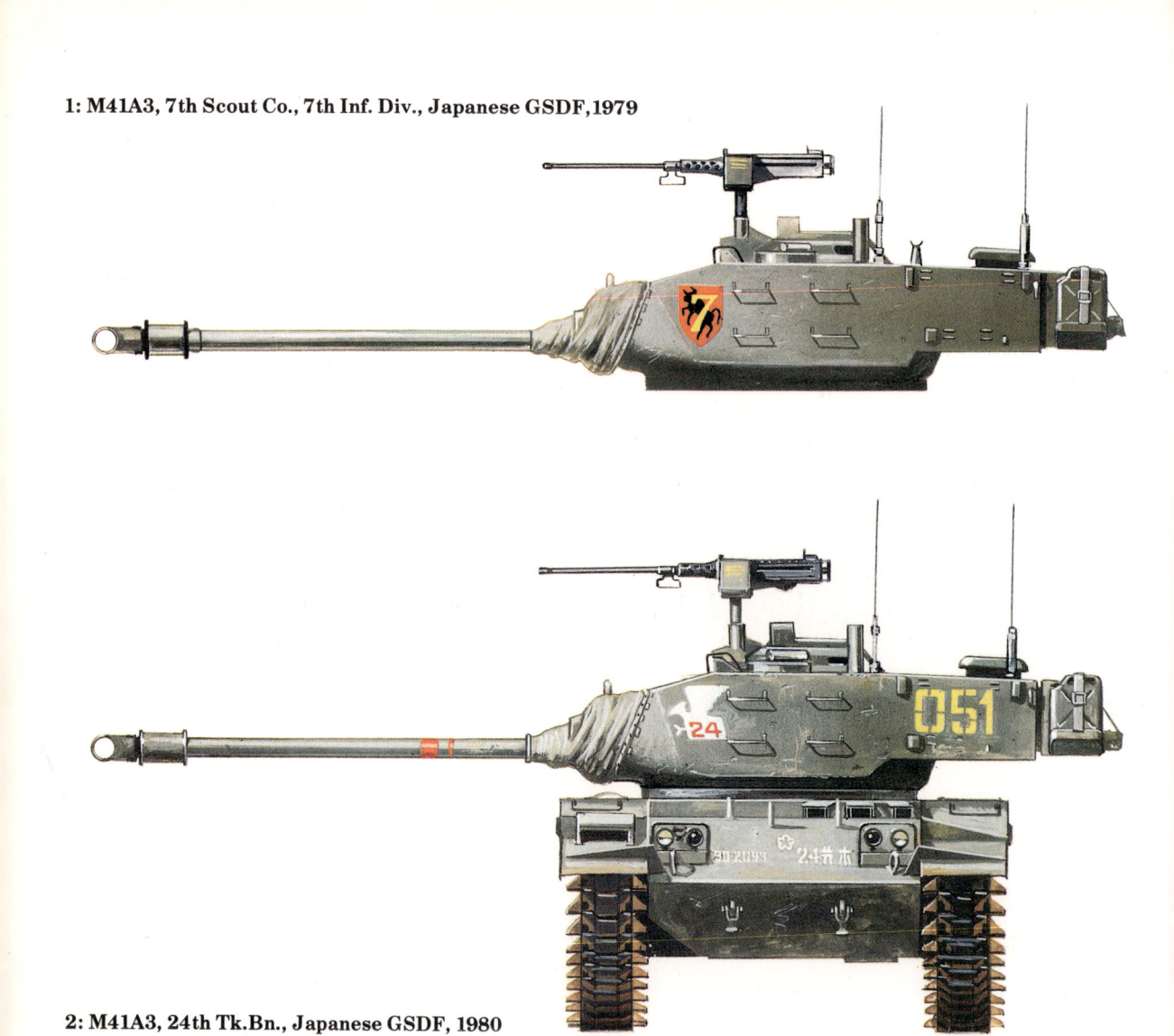

1: M41A3, 7th Scout Co., 7th Inf. Div., Japanese GSDF, 1979

2: M41A3, 24th Tk.Bn., Japanese GSDF, 1980

3: M41A3, 3rd Co., 13th Tk.Bn., Japanese GSDF, 1982

D

1: M41A1, Royal New Zealand Armoured Corps, 1980

2: M41A3, ARVN Armor School; Thu Duc, Vietnam, 1971

E

1: M41A3, Brazilian Army, 1975

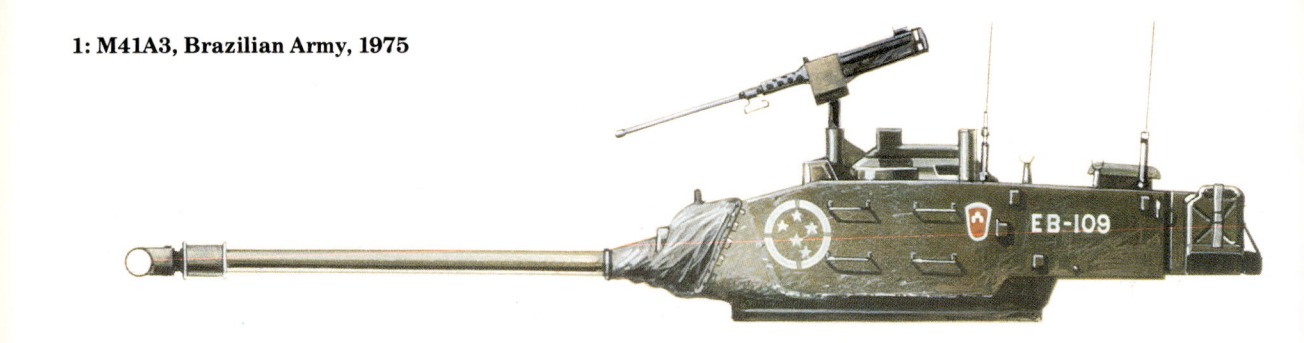

2: M41A1, US 40th Tk.Bn.; Ft.Richardson, Alaska, 1961

3: M41A3, RVN Presidential Gd. Bde.; Saigon, Vietnam, 1968

F

1: M551, US 3/4th Cavalry; Vietnam, 1969

2: M551, US 1/11th Cavalry; Vietnam, 1969

G

1: **M551A1, US 7th Army; Fed. Republic of Germany, 1976**

2: **M551A1, US 4/64th Armor, 82nd Airborne Div., 1981**

H

has repeatedly baulked at financing the Army M1047 programme, but has shown very little awareness of the applicability of the M551 to the same role. The M551 has been experimentally fitted with a trunnion-mounted 75mm autocannon as part of the ELKE (Elevated Kinetic Energy Gun) programme, and with a low-pressure 105mm anti-tank gun. The M551 may yet be resurrected.

Foreign Use of US Light Tanks

The M24 and M41 series were widely exported by the US under the MAP programmes to help build up allied armies, and proved exceedingly popular in this role. They were not very expensive, and they were easy for small armies with little tank experience to maintain. They have seen a fair amount of combat since 1945—though it must also be added that in certain Third World countries they have been used more often as 'voting machines' by military cliques, and have seen frequent use in coups, or by counter-coup forces. The chart below provides some idea of the extent to which these vehicles were exported. It should be kept in mind that the figures for the export of the M24 are less reliable than those for the M41, as records for the late 1940s and early 1950s are not readily available.

Foreign use of M24 & M41

Country	M24	M41	M41A1	M41A2	M41A3
Argentina					50
Austria	54	42			
Belgium	130	84	110		
Brazil		40		83	165
Cambodia	36				
Chile					50
Denmark			53		
Ecuador					25
Ethiopia	34	27	27		17
France	1,254				
Greece	170				100
Iran	180		42		
Iraq	78				
Italy	50				
Japan		46	147		
Laos	4				

This Danish Army tank is an M41A1, but it is almost impossible to distinguish sub-types of this series from photos—all major differences were internal. (Danish Army)

Country	M24	M41	M41A1	M41A2	M41A3
Lebanon		18			
Netherlands	50		50		
New Zealand			10		
Norway	72				
Pakistan	282				
Philippines		7			
Portugal	16		1		
Saudi Arabia	52	36	39		
Spain	180	38			140
Sudan					55
Taiwan	292	207	198	10	373
Thailand	20	93	34	2	141
Tunisia		14	5		
Turkey	114				
Uruguay	17				
S. Vietnam	32				506
United Kingdom	289				
USSR	2				

US Light Tanks in Combat

In view of the large numbers of M24s and M41s exported, it is not surprising that many have been used in the constant wars, coups and border clashes that have marred the tense peace of the past 40 years. Details of the employment of some of these vehicles are not known. For example, both Cambodia and Laos had small numbers of M24s, probably left over from the French. There are few known details about their part in the fighting there in the 1960s. Both Iran and Iraq have also had US

25

South Vietnamese tank squadrons were too frequently used in static defence, like this M41A3 of the 1st Cav. Regt. in August 1968. Once the ARVN officer corps became less political in the late 1960s, they were used more actively in combat. (Lt.Col. James Loop)

light tanks, but there is little evidence that they have been employed in the most recent war in the Gulf.

France France was the largest single foreign recipient of M24 tanks, and indeed was supplied with over a quarter of the total production run. These tanks were first delivered to France in 1950 after the outbreak of the Korean War, when the US took a more favourable attitude towards French activities in Indo-China. Subsequently, the M24 was sent to Indo-China in some numbers to replace the M5A1 Stuart, which was then the principal French tank in use against the Viet Minh. Probably the most famous of the units to use the M24 in large numbers was the *1er Regiment de Chasseurs à Cheval*, which substituted M24s for M5A1s early in 1951. This unit popularly referred to the M24 as the 'Bison'. Initially, French armoured units were organised as they had been in France. It was quickly appreciated that this was unsuitable for the

The Belgian firm of Cockerill proposed to extend the life of the M41 by substituting this improved Mk IV 90mm low-pressure gun for the original 76mm weapon. (Cockerill)

terrain of Indo-China; and in 1951 the first *sous groupements blindées* (GB) were organised. These had a single company of M24s and two mechanised infantry companies in half-tracks. The tank companies had 13 M24s, and eight or nine half-tracks, organised into four platoons each with three M24s and two half-tracks, plus a company command tank. The M24s were used mainly to provide fire support for the mobile infantry, escorting them along the few passable roads.

The M24 proved a godsend for the French forces, as its low ground pressure enabled it to traverse even the marshy ground and rice paddies. The 75mm gun also was much superior to the 37mm gun on the old M5A1, which did not have a very large HE filler. One of the main problems with the 75mm gun on the M24 was that most of the ammunition had super-quick fuses, which meant that it often exploded on hitting virtually anything, including bamboo, overhanging vegetation and other obstructions in front of the main target. The M24 was also wider than the M5A1, and this sometimes caused trouble when moving through narrow village streets. Besides their employment with these infantry support companies in the GBs, the M24s were also assigned to the *groupes d'escadrons de reconnaissance* (GER). Usually these scout groups consisted of a squadron of M24s, an armoured car troop of 15 or 16 M8s, and a platoon of three 75mm Howitzer Motor Carriages for fire support. Usually these GERs operated with a battalion-sized infantry formation on area control operations.

The employment of the M24 in Indo-China was quite varied. It was most commonly used to support infantry attacks, but it also saw service as a convoy escort, for road patrols and for static defence of important bridges or other facilities. The convoy and road patrol duties were the least liked. The Viet Minh were very poorly equipped with anti-tank weapons, so preferred ambushes in close-grained terrain where anti-tank teams could sneak near the

An M551 of Troop A, 3/4th Cavalry on patrol in July 1969; during the squadron's service in Vietnam the 3/4th was assigned to the 25th Infantry Division. The squadron switched to the Sheridan from the popular M48A3, and was not overjoyed at the change. The new tank's vulnerability to mines was accompanied by reliability problems. The improvised external stowage racks are a reminder of the Sheridan's cramped interior. (US Army)

Another massively-stowed Sheridan, this one a tank of Troop E, 1st Cavalry patrolling south of the DMZ on 25 March 1971. At this date the troop was attached to the 11th Inf. Bde. of the 23rd Inf. Div., 'Americal'. By 1971 the M551 had become the standard cavalry tank in Vietnam. This example displays a typical variety of cartoons and slogans. (US Army)

tanks with explosive satchels or Molotov cocktails. Regular road patrols or convoys obviously facilitated the planning of these ambushes, and the lack of passable terrain on either side of the road often channelled the tanks along very narrow paths. This was hardly the sort of mission the speedy M24 had been designed for; but even so, its firepower often turned the tables on the ambushers. For example, on 25 October 1953, the Viet Minh ambushed a 1er RCC column on the road near Lai Cae. In the ensuing fight 180 Viet Minh were killed for only modest French losses. As a result of increasing French finesse in countering such ambushes, most M24 losses came from mines rather than other anti-tank weapons. Indeed, mine losses probably accounted for over 85 per cent of tank casualties.

In 1953 the armoured units were re-organised to take advantage of the improvement in French tactics. The main new formation was the armoured group, also sometimes called the armoured task force. Four of these were formed. They consisted of one company of M24 tanks, three companies of truck-mounted infantry and one mechanised infantry company on half-tracks. Nominally, the tank company consisted of three platoons with five tanks each plus two command tanks, but in practice, there were usually four platoons (one for each infantry company) and only one command tank. The main drawback of the armoured task forces was that the trucks were not as mobile as the nimble M24, and so the whole force was apt to be less mobile. These task forces were considered part of the French strategic reserve and could be assigned to various regions for operations. They proved highly effective in combat. These units should be distinguished from the *Groupements Mobiles*, which usually only had a platoon of three M24 tanks. Some later had a full company of tanks added, but these were often the inferior M5A1.

Probably the most famous use of the M24 took place in December 1953 when ten M24s were transported by air into Dien Bien Phu to support the French 'airhead' being established there. The only transports available, the C-47 and Bristol, could not carry an intact M24, so they had to be broken down into 180 components and re-assembled at Dien Bien Phu. During the fighting of spring 1954 the 'Bisons' were used as mobile artillery batteries, firing about 15,000 rounds during the course of the battle. This caused serious problems with the gun recoil system. Nevertheless, the 'Bisons' soldiered on until Dien Bien Phu was finally overwhelmed in May 1954, when their crews destroyed them to prevent them falling into Viet Minh hands.

Although this was the most famous use of airlifted tanks, it was not the only example. A platoon of five M24s was airlifted into Luang Prabang in Laos; and a company of M5A1s and M8 HMCs was brought into the Plain of Jars for the fighting there.

When French armoured units were repatriated to France in 1954–55, a proportion of the M24s were left behind for the small armoured force being formed in South Vietnam.

Ethiopia Ethiopia was equipped by the US with both M24s and M41s before it began to veer into the Soviet orbit. In the late 1970s the M41s were used alongside Soviet-supplied T-55s against the Eritrean Liberation Front in the Ogaden Desert.

Lebanon The Lebanese Army was supplied with 18 M41s. These were used by government forces in the 1975 civil war, but appear to have fallen into the hands of various factions. It is not clear if the tanks are still operational, or which of the multitude of militias and private armies now control them.

The M551 proved more acceptable in its intended role when finally shipped to Central Europe in the early 1970s. It continued to suffer from problems connected with excessive recoil when firing caseless ammunition, however; and was withdrawn from all except one battalion at the end of the decade. As short-lived was the black beret worn by US Army tankers of the period. (US Army)

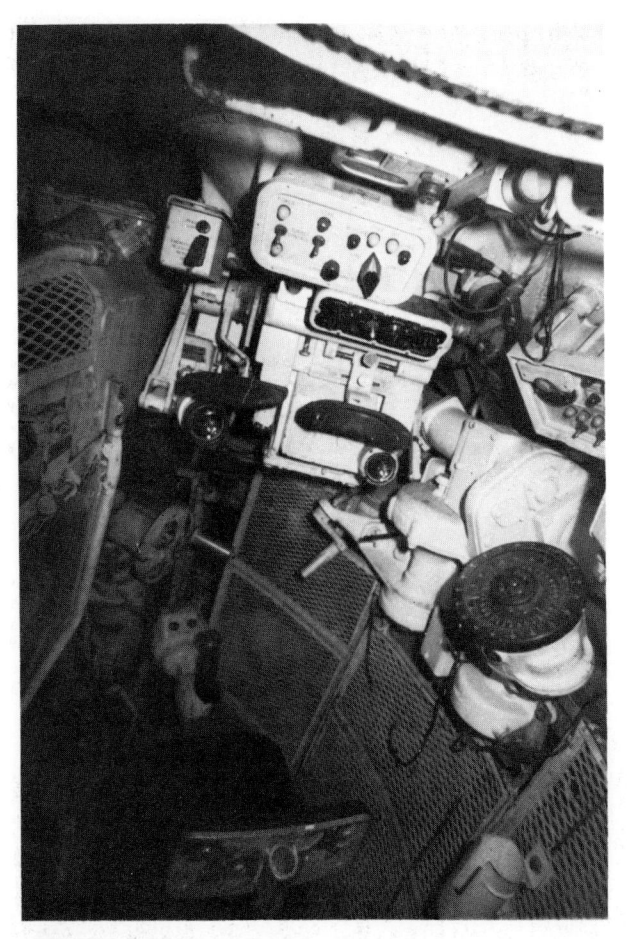

A view of the gunner's station in an M551A1 Sheridan. In the centre are the main controls for aiming the gun/missile launcher and traversing the turret. (Zaloga)

The Cavalry was saddled with two 'lemons' in the 1970s—the M551 and the M114. The latter's main problem was poor track design, which degraded mobility on rough or slippery terrain. These two vehicles are on exercise at Ft. Hood, Texas, in 1975. (Brian Gibbs)

South Vietnam In 1955, after the withdrawal of French forces from Indo-China, the South Vietnamese Army retained four armoured regiments, equipped mostly with armoured cars and half-tracks. In 1956 the US began to supply advisers, and to train Vietnamese officers at the Armor School at Ft. Knox. The four units were re-organised as armoured cavalry regiments, and each had a squadron of M24 tanks—partly ex-French, partly supplied by the US. The total number of M24s in South Vietnam is not known but probably amounted to about 75, with about 15 in each ACR squadron, and the remainder at the Thu Duc Armor School.

The M24s were not extensively used against the Viet Cong in the early days of the Vietnam War. Indeed, the first major combat operation by ARVN M24s occurred on 2 November 1963, when Chaffees of the Armor School and other armoured units fought it out with a smaller number of M24s of the presidential guard brigade during the coup agaist Diem. The M24s were used again on 30 January 1964 to support Gen. Khanh's coup. Not surprisingly, ARVN tank troops soon came to be called 'coup troops' and their M24 tanks 'voting machines'. The use of tanks as decisive factors in these rebellions led the leaders of subsequent successful coups to emasculate the armoured units by assigning commanding officers more notable for their political loyalty than their military ability. The politicisation of the armoured force continued until about 1968, and severely hampered the development of ARVN tank units.

In 1963, with US assistance, the ARVN formed two new units which would eventually become the 5th and 6th Armored Cavalry Regiments. The 5th ACR was in fact the first ARVN tank regiment. However, there were not enough Chaffees to flesh out the new units, and the M24s were suffering from age and a lack of spare parts; and in 1964 the US agreed to re-equip the ARVN armoured cavalry units with M41A3s. These began to arrive in January 1965, and by the end of the year five squadrons had been equipped and trained. Most of the M24s were assigned to airports and other important installations, where they were used as pillboxes for perimeter defence. The engines were removed—not only because of the lack of spares, but also to prevent their use in coups. The only

M24s to remain operational were a small number at Tan Son Nhut airport with Vietnamese Air Force crews. These had been retained as a counter-coup force by Air Marshal Ky, to prevent the use of ARVN tanks against his regime.

The first major use of ARVN tanks took place in October 1965, when an armoured task force was sent to relieve the Plei Me Special Forces Camp. US advisers were critical of the employment of M41s in this operation. Main gun fire was rapid but poorly aimed; the tanks tended to be used nervously and in a static fashion; there was little co-ordination with the M113 APCs, and the tanks tended to bunch up. One of the few bright spots was the fact that ARVN maintenance was excellent, and none of the squadron's 15 tanks were lost. In 1966 the US agreed to expand the ARVN training programme and to enlarge the force to 16 armoured cavalry regiments with 16 squadrons of M41A3 tanks, 15 tanks to a squadron. Nevertheless, the bulk of

As befitted a scout vehicle, the M551 was designed to be amphibious. A screen was contained in hull recesses, and could be erected before entering the water; propulsion was by means of the tracks. This early production vehicle, photographed on trials, is still fitted with the bore evacuator and open-breech scavenger system. (US Army)

An M551A1 photographed during the 'Reforger' exercises in Germany, 1978; in that year the Sheridan began to be withdrawn from US units in Europe due to its chronic problems. This tank has a pyrotechnic display on the front of the main gun tube. The '27-on-orange' panel is an exercise marking—the 'opposing army' uses pale blue panels. (Pierre Touzin)

Interior of the M551 turret, looking from the commander's station forward and left towards the loader's station. The unconventional breech design is very evident in this view. (Zaloga)

armoured fighting by the ARVN rested on the shoulders of the M113 APC mechanised infantry squadrons, as the tank squadrons were often kept close to base to protect high-ranking officers or to prevent their use in mutinies and coups.

As the tank squadrons became depoliticised after 1968 they came to play a more important role in the fighting. The first major tank-vs.-tank confrontation of the Vietnam War took place in February 1971, when the ARVN attacked into Laos to disrupt the Ho Chi Minh Trail. The operation, 'Lam Son 719', included the 1st Armor Brigade and the 11th and 17th Armored Cavalry Regiments. The two units were under strength, with less than 17 tanks. NVA forces in the region had an entire tank battalion, and brought in a portion of a tank regiment to resist the ARVN attack. Heavy NVA attacks against Landing Zone 31 led to the 11th and 17th Armored Cavalry being sent to relieve ARVN airborne units. On 19 February 1971 an M41A3 of 1/11th Armored Cavalry destroyed a T-54. In a fierce, day-long fight, six T-54s and 16 PT-76s were destroyed without loss among the M41s. Nevertheless, after six days of heavy fighting the ARVN units were forced away from LZ31 and the NVA continued to attack the retreating units. On 27 February the NVA attack was again bolstered by armour, but 12 PT-76s and three T-54s were lost to the M41s and tactical airstrikes. Another major NVA armour attack on 1 March led to the loss of 15 NVA tanks for six M113 ACAVs of the ARVN.

Although NVA and ARVN armour did not have any further serious clashes, the ARVN units lost a large percentage of vehicles during the retreat because of harsh terrain conditions, mechanical breakdowns, and a general lack of support for the retreating armoured cavalry units. 'Lam Son 719' represented the only large tank-vs.-tank confrontations before the battles in 1975. It was the largest single use of ARVN armour, involving some six tank squadrons at one point or another (though no more than three squadrons were operational at any one time). The operation was illustrative of the superior training and combat skills of the ARVN tankers compared to the NVA crews, who performed very poorly in the tank-vs.-tank engagements in Laos.

NVA armour was not the only threat to ARVN tanks. On 23 April 1972 the M41 squadron of the 14th Armored Cavalry was wiped out at Tan Canh by a barrage of the new 9M14M *Malyutka* ('Sagger') missiles. This loss was all the more tragic as the NVA launched a major tank attack in that sector shortly afterwards. Due to the extensive use of T-54 and T-55 tanks in the 1972 offensive, the US began supplying the ARVN with M48A3s. Nevertheless, the M41 remained numerically the most common ARVN tank up to the time of the NVA offensive in 1975. The role of the M41 squadrons in the final fighting in April 1975 is little known, although these units were certainly heavily involved in the defence of the Saigon region. NVA units also used modest numbers of captured M41s during the April 1975 fighting.

Pakistan The Pakistani Army used the Chaffee in both the 1965 and 1971 wars with India. The M24 does not appear to have played a significant role in 1965, and reportedly only one was lost. In 1971 its employment was more apparent. The 29th Cavalry, stationed in Bangladesh, had the only Pakistani armour in the eastern region. It possessed 72 M24s, but by this date, the tanks were in very bad shape: the gun tubes were badly worn, which seriously degraded both their range and accuracy. The unit was not kept intact, being broken down into squadrons which were doled out to provide fire support for various Pakistani infantry units. They were faced by far larger numbers of Indian PT-76 and T-55 tanks. Many of the M24s fell to Indian recoilless rifle anti-tank teams, and others to Indian tanks. The M24 was hopelessly out-matched by the T-55, and did not have the gun range of the PT-76. All of the regiment's M24s were lost or surrendered.

Cuba In April 1961 when the CIA-sponsored *Brigada Asalto 2506* landed at the Bay of Pigs in Cuba, they were supported by five M41 tanks of the 4th (Armored) Battalion. The tanks were landed by LCUs on the beach near Giron, and were doled out to provide fire support for the rebel Cuban infantry. The CIA believed the Cuban armour was limited to a small number of IS-3 Stalin tanks, and some M3 Stuart and M4 Sherman tanks from the Batista days. In fact, Castro had received several dozen T-34/85s and SU-100s from Czechoslovakia in the months before the invasion, and a column of these was dispatched towards the Bay of Pigs when Castro learned of the landings. The area around the invasion beaches was poorly suited for armour, being mainly coastal swampland with only a small number of poor sand paths. Around midnight on 17 April, after a day of fighting, the first Castro tanks appeared. An ambush was set up, and two out of three tanks were destroyed at point blank range by the M41s and recoilless rifles. The third swung around the wrecks of the first two. (Although rebel Cuban sources called the opposing vehicles Stalin tanks, in fact they were probably SU-100 assault guns.) Before the SU-100 could fire, it was repeatedly rammed by a rebel M41 which was too close to use its own gun. The M41 sheared off part of the SU-100's gun barrel, and the assault gun retreated with a broken track. Castro's forces made repeated attacks with tanks, but lost several more in other sectors to bazookas and 57mm recoilless rifles. On Wednesday 19 April a large column tried to overrun rebel positions in Giron, but were halted by M41 fire, losing three SU-100s or T-34/85s and one

In the early 1980s a number of M551s were converted to M551A2s for use as Opposing Force (OPFOR) training tanks at the National Training Center in California. This M551A2 has sheet metal additions, in a not altogether convincing attempt to mimic a Soviet BMP. The fabric strip along the turret sides contains the MILES laser detectors used for monitoring wargames combat. (Michael Green)

In lieu of light tanks, the US Army is currently planning to use a derivative of the Marine LAV, the M1047, in its new Mobile Protected Gun battalions. Congress has been wary of providing funding due to the controversy surrounding this programme. This particular LAV is a specially modified version with twin TOW missile launchers added; it was displayed to US Army and Dept. of Defense officials in 1983 in the hope of bolstering support for the programme. (Zaloga)

BTR-152. The Walker Bulldogs proved very handy in providing fire support to rebel units, but began to run out of ammunition. One was lost to artillery or tank fire, and with the collapse of the rebel positions the others were finally scuttled by their crews.

Light Tanks Live On

Given their age, it is surprising to note that many M24s and M41s are still in service, and are likely to remain so for another decade. This is due in part to a number of tank modernisation programmes being conducted worldwide. In 1975 the Norwegian firm of Thune-Eureka began modernising 54 old M24s to the new NM-116 standards. In place of the older engines a Detroit Diesel 6V53T was added (the same engine as in the M113A1 APC). The original 75mm gun was replaced with a French D/925 90mm low-pressure gun and a .50cal. was substituted for the old .30cal. co-axial machine gun. Extensive interal modifications were also made, including a turret basket and replacement of the bow machine gunner's station with an additional ammunition rack. The Norwegian Army vehicles also had a Simrad LV3 laser rangefinder added for greater long-range accuracy. This extensive rebuilding was undertaken in part because the Norwegians were content with the durability of the M24, and they felt that the cost of the modernisation amounted to less than a third the cost of a comparable new tank. Interestingly enough, the Norwegians also converted a small number of the remaining M24s into light armoured recovery vehicles.

Napco Industries in the US subsequently obtained licence rights for the modernisation package, and so other countries may modernise their M24s in this fashion. Greece was given a demonstration of the modernised M24, but felt it could undertake the project on its own without US assistance. Using engines which became surplus when its M113s were converted to M113A1 standard, the Greeks tried a similar conversion. It was unsuccessful; and the M24s are reportedly now used as static shore defence points until the Greek Army decides whether it wishes to pay for a complete rebuilding like the NM-116. Taiwan is re-engining its M24s with the Napco powerpack conversion, but apparently not the gun.

Likewise, the M41 has been the subject of a number of modernisation efforts. In Spain M41s are being rebuilt using another Napco offering, which involves replacement of the old engine by a new Detroit Diesel 8V71T as used on the M109 and M110 self-propelled guns. About half of the Walker Bulldogs are expected to remain as tanks with their 76mm gun and possibly with new Cadillac Gage turret power controls. The remainder are expected to be converted into tank destroyers armed with guided anti-tank missiles. At the time of writing Spain had not decided whether to proceed with a TOW system or a HOT missile system. The tank destroyer conversion was developed by Talbot SA in Spain. The TOW type consists of a heavily re-worked hull and Napco re-engining, with an Emerson Electric TOW Under Armor (TUA) elevated trunnion launcher as used on the US M901 ITV. The resulting vehicle has been nicknamed the Cazador. A similar conversion has been developed for the HOT, though without the elevated trunnion mounting.

Brazil has undertaken a similar programme called the M41B. The M41B was developed by Bernardini using a licence-produced Saab Scania DS-14 400hp diesel. Besides these re-engining efforts, the Belgian firms of PRB and Cockerill jointly developed a new main gun for the M41, the NR8510 Mk IV 90mm low-pressure gun. At least 22 of these conversions have been undertaken for Uruguay. It is quite likely that other countries which still have holdings of M24s and M41s will embark on similar re-engining and rebuilding efforts. The M24 and M41 are sturdy, reliable vehicles, and rebuilding offers a very cost-effective alternative to the purchase of entirely new tanks.

The Plates

A1: M24, US 79th Tank Battalion; Han River, Korea, 1950
The 79th Battalion painted many of its tanks with tiger faces, in a peculiar attempt to instil fear in their allegedly superstitious Chinese adversaries. These schemes were applied to both their M4A3E8 Shermans and to 'A' Company's M24s, as shown here. The bumper codes, 25-79△ A-12, indicate that the battalion was attached to the 25th Infantry Division.

A2: M24, 1er Régiment de Chasseurs à Cheval; Indo-China, 1953
French Chaffees were usually left in the overall olive drab delivery scheme. Markings here include the 1er RCC regimental badge painted full-colour on the left side of the turret. Inset is the traditional French tank squadron marking, in this case a red heart on a white square, painted on the right side of the tureet in the same position. The individual number '5' is in white. On the bow plate are the vehicle name, METZ; the serial number, prefixed as usual by a small tricolour flash; and the yellow bridging circle. The name and serial are backed by black rectangles. The serial was repeated, in the same fashion, on the lower rear edge of the turret stowage bin.

B1: M24, 3rd Tank Battalion, Japanese Ground Self-Defence Force, 1970
In the 1970s Japanese GSDF tank units began using colourful insignia: some, like the yellow and red scorpion of the 3rd Tank Battalion, were applied to entire units, while others differed at company level.

B2: M24, South Korean Army Tank Training Center; Kwang-ju, 1953
The ROK Army was initially provided with small numbers of M36 tank destroyers, and later with the M24. Only after the war were Korean tanks normally marked with the ROK national insignia illustrated here.

B3: M24, Escadron de Marche du 1er RCC; Dien Bien Phu, March 1954
The 'Bisons' were camouflage-painted by their crews after their re-assembly. The few photos which survive of the tanks during the siege of Dien Bien Phu show that some were painted with earth yellow stripes, and others with what seem to be earth yellow and red-brown—the latter almost certainly local mud. The size and pattern of the camouflage stripes differed widely from tank to tank: most seem to have favoured a dense pattern of small, basically diagonal slashes, but photos of CONTI suggest these large, random areas of yellow. Tank names were

Finally replacing the M551 in armoured cavalry regiments is the Bradley Fighting Vehicle. The M2 version is for the infantry, and carries more troops; the cavalry's M3 carries two scouts in the hull, with extra ammunition for the main armament, and has no firing ports for the rear compartment. (Zaloga)

painted in white capitals on the turret sides; the lettering was quite crude in some cases, but CONTI displays neat stencilling in the usual French thick/thin style. This was the mount of the squadron commander, the heroic Capt. Yves Hervouët; wounded first in one and then in the other arm, he continued to lead counter-attacks with both arms in plaster. (He survived the siege, but not the Viet Minh death-camps.) Note the infantry radio propped on the far side of the rear deck, and the spare ammunition tubes on the trackguards—both features shown in photos of CONTI. The 'Bisons' often fired 60 to 100 rounds in an action, and the internal load of 48 rounds was quite inadequate. This tank was badly damaged on 5 April during a counter-attack at strongpoint 'Huguette 6'; it was recovered, and used as a static pillbox south of the airstrip for the rest of the siege.

C1: M24, South Vietnamese Air Force Security Flight; Tan Son Nhut airfield, RVN, 1968

After the ARVN was re-equipped with M41s, the only M24s to remain fully operational were the

The XM800 ARSV was an attractive light scout tank design developed by FMC to replace the ill-fated M114. It was cancelled, however, and the M114/M551 replacement programme was merged with the M2 IFV/M3 CFV programme. (FMC Corp.)

A shape of things to come? In the late 1970s/early 1980s, AAI Corp. developed a number of light tanks from the experimental HSTV-L testbed in the hope of interesting the US Army and Marines in their procurement for the Rapid Deployment Force. This tank is armed with a revolutionary 75mm Ares XM274 automatic cannon. Tanks like this are being proposed for the Army's Mobile Protected Gun programme, which aims to field a new light tank in the 1990s. (AAI Corp.)

Air Force tanks which served as a precautionary counter-coup force for Premier Ky. They were camouflaged in olive drab, forest green and earth red. This tank was named after Vic Morrow, the TV actor who played in the popular series 'Combat'. Some of these Chaffees also appear to have displayed a large red insignia painted on the roof, but details are lacking.

C2: M24, Mecklenbourg Cavalry Regiment, Portuguese 1st Independent Mixed Brigade, 1978

This colourfully-marked Chaffee served with the Portuguese armoured cavalry until retired in the early 1980s. The scheme is a pattern of sand yellow and earth red over the basic olive drab. The regiment's crest is painted on the turret side; the front fender markings are the arm-of-service flashes of the brigade and regiment. A cavalry regiment of this name has served with the Portuguese army since the 18th century.

D1: M41A3, 7th Scout Tank Company, Japanese GSDF, 1979

The scout companies attached to Japanese infantry divisions often use a different insignia from that of the division's attached tank battalion. In the case of the 7th Infantry Division both the scout company and tank battalion use variations of the stylised '7', but in the scout unit it is marked on a red shield.

D2: M41A3, 24th Tank Battalion, Japanese GSDF, 1980

This battalion uses a stylised eagle insignia with the battalion number. Many battalions also use turret tactical numbers, as here. Hull front markings are the vehicle serial (left), the unit identification (right), and the traditional national *oka* or cherry blossom insignia (centre).

37

AAI Corp. also developed a derivative of its RDF/LT with the same 76mm gun as the M41 tank, intended for export—the US would not allow overseas sales of the new Ares 75mm automatic cannon. (AAI Corp.)

D3: M41A3, 3rd Tank Company, 13th Tank Battalion, Japanese GSDF, 1982
The 13th is one of the most colourfully-marked Japanese tank battalions. Each company has a different insignia; in the case of the 3rd it is this splendidly gaudy dragon.

E1: M41A1, Royal New Zealand Armoured Corps, 1980
The Walker Bulldog was used in limited numbers by the RNZAC until finally retired in 1983. In the late 1970s they were camouflaged as shown here, in a pattern of dark green, rust brown, black and sand distributed in a scheme very similar to those of the US Army.

E2: M41A3, ARVN Armor School; Thu Duc, RVN, 1971
The Armor School was one of the few South Vietnamese tank units to display an insignia on its vehicles. This stylised elephant motif was carried on both sides of the turret. The vehicle serial number was marked on the lower bow and lower rear plate on a chrome yellow rectangle; 'TG' was marked on a circle on the right fender.

F1: M41A3, Brazilian Army, 1975
The Brazilian Army uses the traditional national insignia, the 'Big Dipper' or 'Great Bear' in a circle. The vehicle serial 'EB-109' (Brazilian Army 109) is carried on the turret side, together with the tank unit's crest.

F2: M41A1, US 40th Tank Battalion; Fort Richardson, Alaska, 1961
The 40th Tank Battalion was used extensively in Arctic wargames in Alaska, and frequently played the part of Aggressor forces. The green triangle within a white circle was the insignia adopted for Aggressor units. During winter exercises the tanks were camouflaged with whitewash sprayed in swathes over the base colour.

F3: M41A3, Republic of Vietnam Presidential Guard Brigade; Saigon, 1968
This M41 carries a white lightning-bolt, and the name VU BAO ('Resolute Tiger'). A small number of Walker Bulldogs were stationed at the Presidential Palace as an anti-coup force after the earlier M24s were knocked out in the 1963 fighting. They were also used for parades in the capital.

G1: M551, US 3/4th Cavalry, Republic of Vietnam, 1969
The 3rd Sqn. of the US 4th Armored Cavalry Regiment was one of the two squadrons to receive the troubled M551 Sheridan in Vietnam. The insignia consisted of the traditional red/white cavalry guidon, and the vehicle number '36'. As was commonplace in Vietnam, unofficial names were added by the crews—in this case, SUDDEN DEATH. An extensive external stowage is evident on this tank: the Sheridan was notably cramped inside.

G2: M551, US 1/11th Cavalry, Republic of Vietnam, 1969
The turrets of Sheridans in Vietnam quickly acquired not only a purpose-designed 'crow's-nest' or 'bird-cage' of armour plate, but frequently additional machine guns as well—some photos show examples with up to four M60s mounted externally. This tank of C Troop, 1st Sqn., 11 ACR appears to have two white barrel-bands identifying 2 Platoon. On the hull side is the standard type of stencil block, in this case 'U.S. ARMY/12C 80368'; and a vehicle name, CANARY CAGE II. A second slogan has been painted on the 152mm gun barrel—152 INSTAMATIC. There is a good deal of external stowage on the turret, including a string of smoke grenades; apart from the operational necessity of having these close to hand, there was also the odd but vital fact that green smoke grenades—and green ones only!—proved an effective repellent of the savage local bees.

Talbot SA. in Spain developed this *Cazador* ('Hunter') tank destroyer vehicle based on the M41 tank, and the Spanish Army plans to convert about half of its Bulldogs to this configuration; the remainder will be re-engined. The TOW missile launcher on this vehicle is the same type used on the American M901 ITV tank destroyer on the M113 chassis. (Talbot SA)

H1: M551A1, US 7th Army, Federal Republic of Germany, 1976

In the mid-1970s armoured units of the 7th Army in Germany began experimenting with pattern-painted camouflage. These schemes should not be confused with the later, official MERDC schemes which superseded them in the late 1970s. The 7th Army schemes can be distinguished by their wider bands of colour; the lack of distinctive 'crow's-feet' patterns; and the brighter colours—in this case Earth Red, Forest Green, Sand and Black.

H2: M551A1, US 4/64th Armor, 82nd Airborne Division, 1981

The 4/64th is the last American tank battalion still equipped with the Sheridan, and has been the only unit extensively used in the airborne role. This tank is finished in the current MERDC scheme of Forest Green, Field Drab, Sand and Black. On the hull sides is the company symbol—a square—with the vehicle number inside. Standard bumper codes are painted on the bow and rear.

Farbtafeln

A1 Auf den M24-Panzern dieser A-Kompanie sowie auf den Shermans der anderen Kompanien dieser Einheit befanden sich diese aussergewöhnlichen 'Tigergesichter'. Man glaubte fälschlicherweise, sie würden abergläubische, chinesische Truppen einschüchtern. **A2** Die Bezeichnungen 'Metz' und '5' stellen Name und Nummer dieses bestimmten Panzers dar. Auf der linken Geschützseite befindet sich das Regimentsabzeichen des *1er RCC*, auf der rechten Seite die herzförmigen Kompanieinsignien.

B1 Alle Panzer dieses Bataillons waren mit den Skorpioninsignien versehen. **B2** Die koreanischen Nationalzeichen am Geschütz fand man erst nach dem Koreakrieg. **B3** Das ist der Panzer von Capt. Hervouët, dem heldenhaften Kommandant der Panzerschwadron bei Dien Bien Phu. Trotz Verletzungen an beiden Armen führte er zahlreiche Angriffe durch; er starb in Viet Minh-Gefangenschaft. Die Panzer wurden individuell getarnt, entweder mit sandfarbigem Anstrich oder sogar mit rotem Schlamm. Auch die Bezeichnungen am Geschütz waren von Panzer zu Panzer verschieden.

C1 Diese am Saigoner Flugplatz zum Schutz von Premierminister Ky stationierte Einheit hatte als einzige voll einsatzfähige M24-Panzer, nachdem sie bereits durch die M41-Panzer ersetzt worden waren. **C2** Das Regimentswappen befindet sich auf der Geschützseite. Auf der linken und auf der rechten Seite des Kettenschutzes sehen Sie die Brigaden- bzw. Regimentssymbole.

D1 Die Insignien dieser Kompanie bestehen aus einer stilisierten '7' auf einem roten, schildförmigen Hintergrund. Das Panzerbataillon der Division hatte ein ähnliches Abzeichen, jedoch ohne Schild. **D2** Die Insignien dieses Bataillons sind ein stilisierter Adler sowie die Bataillonsnummer. Die Rumpfbezeichnungen sind von links nach rechts wie folgt: die Seriennummer, die traditionelle, japanische Kirschblüte und das Abzeichen der Einheit. **D3** Jede Kompanie dieses Bataillons hat unterschiedliche Insignien.

E1 Die RNZAC verwendete bei den M41 ein ähnliches aber nicht genau dasselbe Tarnschema wie das MERDC-Schema der US Army. **E2** Eine der wenigen ARVN-Einheiten, die ihre Insignien zeigten; hier ein stilisierter Elefant.

F1 Das Sternbild dient als Nationalabzeichen; die Geschützinsignien bestehen aus dem Regimentswappen. **F2** Diese Einheit spielte bei arktischen Manövern den 'Feind'—das dreieckige, grüne Symbol wurde als Zeichen der feindlichen Einheiten übernommen. **F3** Dieser Panzer heisst *Vu Bao*, d.h. 'resoluter Tiger'.

G1 Die Bezeichnung *'Sudden Death'* (plötzlicher Tod) wurde dem Panzer von der Besatzung gegeben. Die traditionelle Kavalleriestandarte befindet sich auf dem Rumpf, ausserdem die Panzernummer '36'. **G2** Die beiden Farbstreifen am Geschütz deuten auf den 2. Zug hin. Der Name auf dem Rumpf, *Canary Cage II* (Vogelkäfig II) sowie der auf dem Geschütz, *152 Instamatic*, sind eine Anspielung auf das Kaliber des Geschützes sowie auf eine gewöhnliche Kamera.

H1 Dieses Versuchs-Tarnschema ist für die 7. Armee Mitte der 70er Jahre typisch, unterscheidet sich aber von den später verwendeten, offiziellen MERDC-Schemen, die es ersetzten. **H2** Das offizielle MERDC-Schema beim letzten Sheridan-Panzerbataillon.

Notes sur les planches en couleur

A1 Les chars M24 de cette compagnie 'A' de l'unité, ainsi que les Shermans des autres compagnies, étaient peints avec ces extraordinaires 'faces de tigre' que l'on pensait à tort devoir effrayer les troupes superstitieuses chinoises. **A2** 'Metz' et '5' sont le nom et le numéro individuel de ce char. L'écusson du régiment *1er RCC* est peint du côté gauche de la tourelle, et l'insigne du 'coeur' de la compagnie se trouve à droite.

B1 Cet insigne de scorpion était porté par tous les chars de ce bataillon. **B2** La marque nationale coréenne sur la tourelle n'a été vue qu'après la fin de la guerre de Corée. **B3** Le char du Capitaine Hervouët, l'héroïque commandant de cet escadron de chars à Dien Bien Phu; il a mené de nombreuses attaques malgré les blessures sur ces deux bras, et est mort lors de sa captivité chez le Viet Minh. Les chars portaient des camouflages individuels, de couleur sable et quelquefois avec de la boue rouge; les noms sur les tourelles montraient aussi les différences de style d'un char à l'autre.

C1 Cette unité, en poste sur le terrain d'aviation de Saigon en tant que force de sécurité du Premier Ky, a été la seule à conserver les chars M24 en bon état de marche après qu'ils aient été remplacés dans les unités blindées par les M41. **C2** L'insigne du régiment est peinte sur le côté de la tourelle; les gardes-boue portent les symboles de la brigade et du régiment des côtés gauche et droit respectivement.

D1 Le '7' stylisé était utilisé comme insigne par cette compagnie sur un bouclier à fond rouge; le bataillon des chars de la division utilisait un marquage semblable sans le bouclier. **D2** Un aigle stylisé et le numéro de bataillon étaient l'insigne du bataillon. Les marquages sur la coque, sont, de gauche à droite: le numéro de série, la fleur de cerisier traditionnelle du Japon, et le symbole de l'unité. **D3** Chaque compagnie de ce bataillon a un insigne différent.

E1 Les M41 RNZAC utilisaient un modèle de camouflage similaire mais non identique au modèle MERDC de l'Armée des Etats-Unis. **E2** L'une des quelques unités ARVN qui montraient un insigne—ici, un éléphant stylisé.

F1 La marquage national est la constellation d'étoiles; l'insigne de tourelle est l'insigne du régiment. **F2** Cette unité a joué le rôle d'ennemi' lors des exercices dans l'Arctique—la marque du triangle vert était adopté pour les unités 'ennemies'. **F3** Le nom de ce char est *'Vu Bao'*, le 'Tigre Résolu'.

G1 Le nom *'Sudden Death'*—'Mort Soudaine'—a été ajouté par l'équipage et n'est pas officiel. L'étendard de cavalerie traditionnel est peint sur la coque, ainsi que le numéro de char individuel '36'. **G2** Les deux cercles peints autour du canon indiquent qu'il s'agit du 2ème Peloton. Le nom inscrit sur la coque est *'Canary Cage II'*—'Cage du Canari II'—et celui qui se trouve sur le canon *'152 Instamatic'* est un calembour sinistre qui porte sur le calibre du canon et le nom d'un appareil photographique populaire et bon marché.

H1 Ce modèle de camouflage expérimental est typique de ceux qui étaient utilisés par la 7ème armée au milieu des années 1970, et est légèrement différent des modèles plus tardifs et officiels MERDC qui les ont remplacés. **H2** Le modèle officiel MERDC qui était porté par le dernier bataillon de chars Sheridan en service.

40